ROMANIAN FOLK DANCES
for ALTO SAXOPHONE

The
BOOSEY & HAWKES
BARTÓK
EDITION

STYLISH ARRANGEMENTS OF SELECTED HIGHLIGHTS
FROM THE LEADING 20TH CENTURY COMPOSER

Arranged by Hywel Davies

Boosey & Hawkes Music Publishers Ltd
www.boosey.com

HYWEL DAVIES

Hywel Davies is an award-winning composer, arranger and creative artist.

His compositions have been performed by a wealth of ensembles including Kokoro (Bournemouth Symphony Orchestra's new music ensemble, with whom he has a long-standing association), and have been broadcast internationally by the BBC, CBC (Canada) and ABC (Australia). In 2003 he was the recipient of an Arts Council England International Fellowship.

As an arranger, Davies has been published by Boosey & Hawkes, Durand-Salabert-Eschig, Chester Music, Novello, the Associated Board of the Royal Schools of Music and Music Sales. Recent projects for Boosey & Hawkes have included two volumes of pieces by Ástor Piazzolla (*El viaje* & *Vuelvo al sur*), and a volume of works by Rachmaninoff (*Play Rachmaninoff*); he has also compiled several anthologies of piano music including most recently *American Greats* and *Ballet & Other Dances* from the *Boosey & Hawkes Solo Piano Collection*.

Davies is in demand as a sonic and installation artist, and has received commissions from organisations including Arts Council England and the National Trust, often working as an Artist in Residence.

www.hyweldavies.co.uk

Published by Boosey & Hawkes Music Publishers Ltd
Aldwych House
71–91 Aldwych
London
WC2B 4HN

www.boosey.com

© Copyright 2016 by Boosey & Hawkes Music Publishers Ltd

ISMN 979-0-060-13203-2
ISBN 978-1-78454-196-5

First impression 2016

Printed by Halstan:
Halstan UK, 2-10 Plantation Road, Amersham, Bucks, HP6 6HJ. United Kingdom
Halstan DE, Weißliliengasse 4, 55116 Mainz. Germany

With thanks to Charlotte Caird for advice
Music origination by Sarah Lofthouse
Cover design by Chloë Alexander Design (chloealexanderdesign.dphoto.com)

ROMANIAN FOLK DANCES
for ALTO SAXOPHONE

Arranged by Hywel Davies

Piano accompaniment

In its original form, *Romanian Folk Dances* is a suite of six short piano pieces which Bartók composed in 1915 and subsequently transcribed for orchestra in 1917. It is based on seven traditional Romanian melodies which would have been played on the violin or flute, and represents six dance forms.

BÉLA BARTÓK

Béla Bartók was born in the Hungarian town of Nagyszentmiklós (now Sînnicolau Mare in Romania) on 25 March 1881, and received his first music lessons from his mother. When his family moved he took further lessons in Pressburg (now Bratislava in Slovakia) before becoming a student at the Royal Academy of Music in Budapest – graduating in 1903. He began to establish an international reputation as a fine pianist, and was soon drawn into teaching: in 1907 he became professor of piano at the Academy.

Bartók's earliest compositions offer a blend of late Romanticism and nationalist elements, formed under the influences of Wagner, Brahms, Liszt and Strauss. Around 1905 his friend and fellow-composer Zoltán Kodály directed his attention to Hungarian folk music and – coupled with his discovery of the music of Debussy – Bartók's musical language changed dramatically. As he absorbed more and more of the spirit of Hungarian folk songs and dances, his own music grew more concentrated, chromatic and dissonant. Although a sense of key is sometimes lost in individual passages, Bartók never espoused atonality as a compositional technique.

Bartók's interest is folk music was not merely passive: he was an assiduous ethnomusicologist, and undertook his first systematic collecting trips in Hungary with Kodály. Thereafter Bartók's interest and involvement grew deeper and his scope wider, encompassing a number of ethnic traditions both near at hand and further afield: Transylvanian, Romanian, North African and others.

In the 1920s and '30s Bartók's international fame spread, and he toured widely, both as pianist (usually in his own works) and as a respected composer. Works like *Dance Suite* for orchestra (1923) and *Divertimento* for strings (1939) maintained his high profile. He continued to teach at the Academy of Music until his resignation in 1934, devoting much of his free time thereafter to his ethnomusicological research.

With the outbreak of the Second World War, and despite his deep attachment to his homeland, life in Hungary became intolerable and Bartók emigrated to the United States. Here his material conditions worsened considerably, despite initial promise: although he obtained a post at Columbia University and was able to pursue his folk-music studies, his concert engagements become very much rarer. He received few commissions, so the request for a Concerto for Orchestra (1943) was therefore particularly important, bringing him much-needed income. Bartók died following a period of ill health on 26 September 1945.

ROMANIAN FOLK DANCES

1. Stick Dance *(Bot-tánc)*

BÉLA BARTÓK
(1881–1945)

4

2. Sash Dance *(Brâul)*

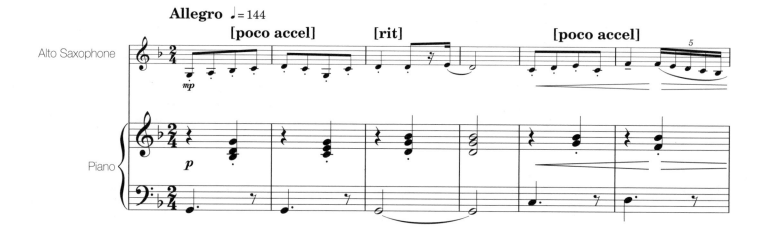

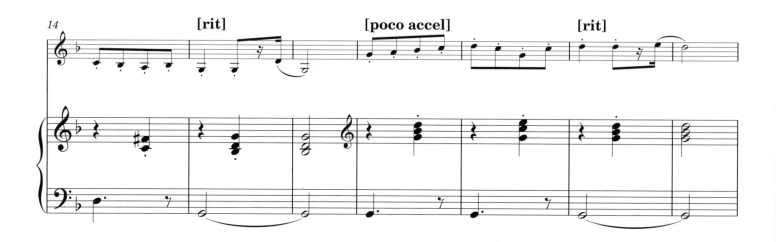

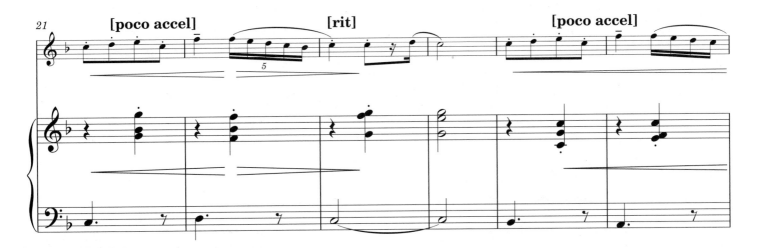

3. In One Spot *(Topogó)*

ROMANIAN FOLK DANCES
for ALTO SAXOPHONE

The ___ ___
BOOSEY & HAWKES
BARTÓK
EDITION

STYLISH ARRANGEMENTS OF SELECTED HIGHLIGHTS
FROM THE LEADING 20TH CENTURY COMPOSER

Arranged by Hywel Davies

ALTO SAXOPHONE IN E♭

BOOSEY & HAWKES

Boosey & Hawkes Music Publishers Ltd
www.boosey.com

Published by Boosey & Hawkes Music Publishers Ltd
Aldwych House
71–91 Aldwych
London
WC2B 4HN

www.boosey.com

© Copyright 2016 by Boosey & Hawkes Music Publishers Ltd

ISMN 979-0-060-13203-2
ISBN 978-1-78454-196-5

First impression 2016

Printed by Halstan:
Halstan UK, 2-10 Plantation Road, Amersham, Bucks, HP6 6HJ. United Kingdom
Halstan DE, Weißliliengasse 4, 55116 Mainz. Germany

With thanks to Charlotte Caird for advice
Music origination by Sarah Lofthouse
Cover design by Chloë Alexander Design (chloealexanderdesign.dphoto.com)

ROMANIAN FOLK DANCES

1. Stick Dance *(Bot-tánc)*

BÉLA BARTÓK
(1881–1945)

2

2. Sash Dance *(Brâul)*

3. In One Spot *(Topogó)*

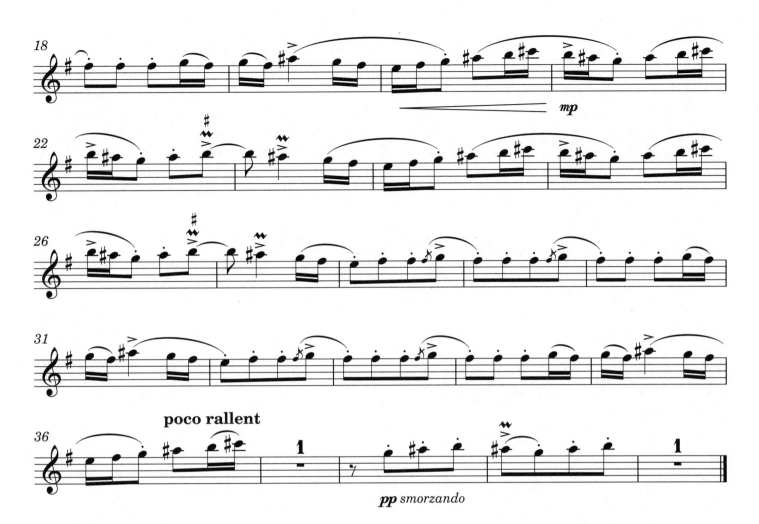

4. Dance from Bucsum *(Bucsumi tánc)*

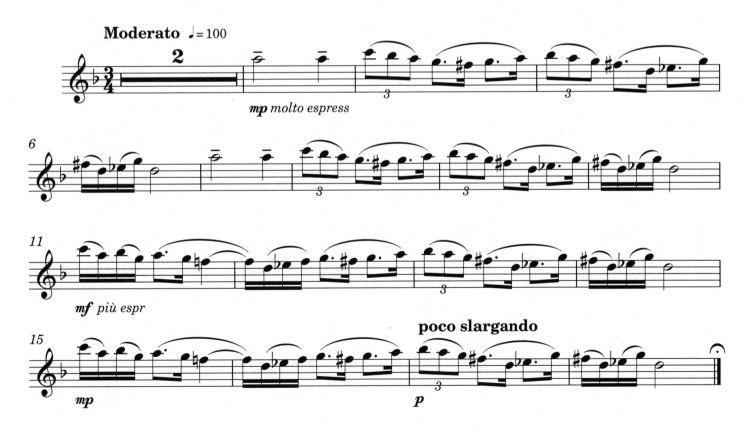

4

5. Romanian Polka *(Román polka)*

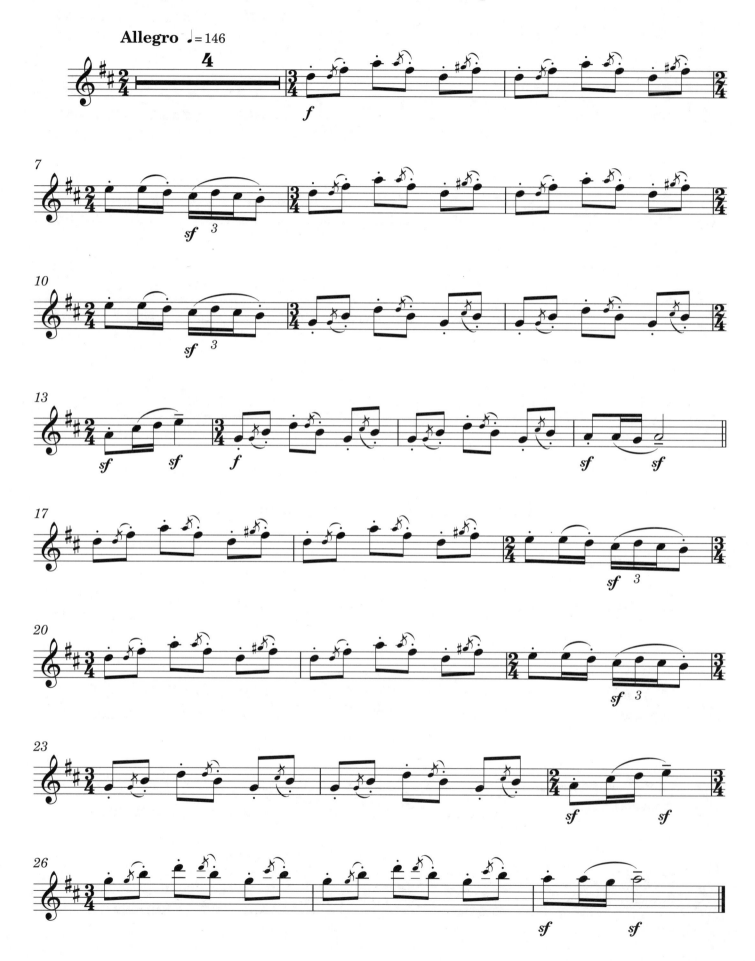

5

6. Fast Dance *(Aprózó)*

4. Dance from Bucsum *(Bucsumi tánc)*

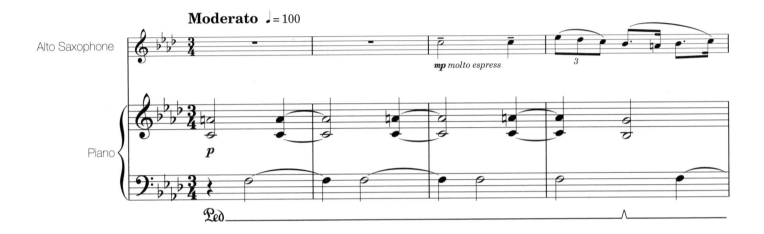

5. Romanian Polka *(Román polka)*

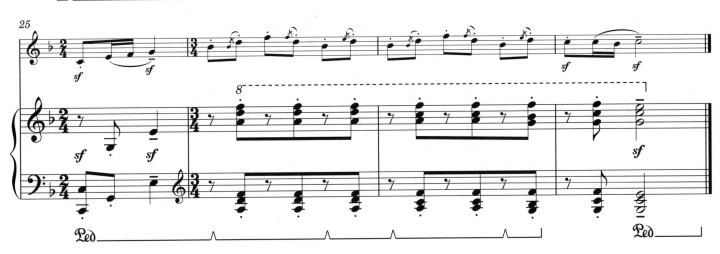

6. Fast Dance *(Aprózó)*

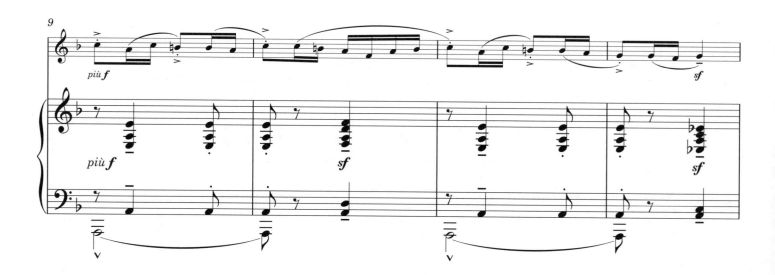

Più allegro ♩ = 152

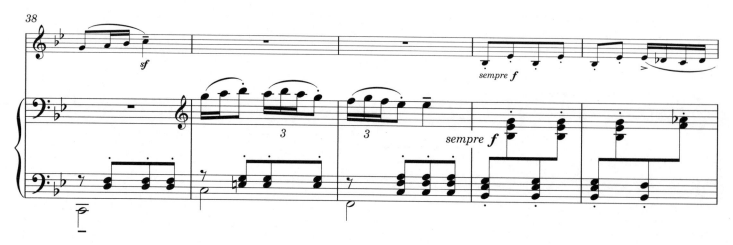

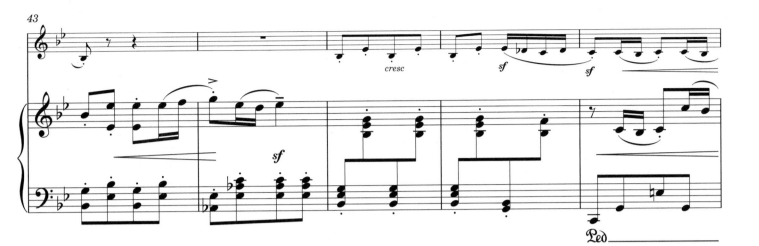